Mary Leads Us to Jesus

*The Marian Spirituality of
Blessed James Alberione, SSP*

Edited with an introduction
by Marianne Lorraine Trouvé, FSP

Pauline
BOOKS & MEDIA
Boston

*Dedicated to my mother,
Lorraine Budris Trouvé,
who gave birth to me on the feast of
Mary's Immaculate Conception
and dedicated me to her.*

The Scripture quotations contained herein are from the *New Revised Standard Version Bible, Catholic Edition,* copyright © 1996 and 1989 by the Division of Christian Education of the National Council of Churches of Christ in the U.S.A. Used by permission. All rights reserved.

Cover photo: FSP–U.S.A. Archives

ISBN 0-8198-4835-2

All rights reserved. No part of this book may be reproduced or transmitted in any form or by any means, electronic or mechanical, including photocopying, recording or by any information storage and retrieval system, without permission in writing from the publisher.

"P" and PAULINE are registered trademarks of the Daughters of St. Paul.

Copyright © 2004, Daughters of St. Paul

Published in the U.S.A. by Pauline Books & Media, 50 Saint Pauls Avenue, Boston, MA 02130-3491.

Printed in Canada

www.pauline.org

Pauline Books & Media is the publishing house of the Daughters of St. Paul, an international congregation of women religious serving the Church with the communications media.

1 2 3 4 5 6 7 8 9   11 10 09 08 07 06 05 04

CONTENTS

Introduction
page v

Editor's Note
page xx

CHAPTER 1

Mary Gives Jesus to Us
page 1

CHAPTER 2

Mary Is the Mother of All Humanity
page 17

CHAPTER 3

Mary, Queen of Apostles
page 31

CHAPTER 4

Mary Our Teacher
page 53

CHAPTER 5

Mary Helps Us to Pray
page 73

Queen of Apostles Basilica, Rome

INTRODUCTION

ROME, APRIL 27, 2003. Outside St. Peter's Square, thousands of pilgrims wait as the crowd swells with the rising excitement. When the guards finally open the gates, the people press forward and pour into the piazza. The Pope is to beatify six holy men and women this morning, including Fr. James Alberione, the founder of the Pauline Family (1884–1971). The pilgrims—priests, men and women religious, and lay persons who belong to the "Pauline Family"—speak Italian, English, French, Spanish, Japanese, Korean, Swahili, Chinese... How did a farm boy from Piedmont, northern Italy, start a movement that has spread so far around the globe? His "secret of success," as he called it, was to trust entirely in divine Providence and to offer everything to the Lord "through the hands of Mary, Queen of the Apostles."

The Night Between the Centuries

JAMES ALBERIONE was born on April 4, 1884, into a devout farming family in Fossano, a small town in Piedmont, northern Italy. From a young age James knew he wanted to be a priest, and he entered the minor seminary. But while there he experienced an adolescent crisis and was asked to leave. After a time he recovered from this blow and his pastor helped him to enter the diocesan seminary of Alba. There, he proved himself. On the night dividing the nineteenth and twentieth centuries, December 31, 1900, sixteen-year-old James had a profound spiritual experience that would mark his life forever. He spent several hours praying during solemn adoration of the Eucharist after Mass. He later recalled:

> A special light came from the Blessed Sacrament, a greater understanding of the invitation extended by Jesus: "Come to me, all of you...." [I] felt deeply obliged to prepare myself to do something for God and the people of the new century in which [I] would live.

Alberione didn't know then where that divine inspiration would lead him, but things would gradually grow clear as he sought God's will. After his ordination, he formed a group of young people to work in an important modern mission: to spread the Gospel *with the media*. He began the Society of St. Paul (priests and brothers) and the Daughters of St. Paul (religious sisters) to work in this mission. He later founded three more religious congregations, four secular institutes, and an association of lay cooperators, collectively known as the Pauline Family. Pope John Paul II said of him:

> In the heart of that chosen priest from the Diocese of Alba beats once again the heart of the Apostle Paul who, won over by Christ, sought to announce him as "the Way, the Truth and the Life." Attentive to the signs of the times, Fr. Alberione did not only open the modern "pulpits" of the media to evangelization, but conceived of his work as an organic action in the Church and at her service.

Alberione developed the charism that God gave him, and it blossomed into a profound spirituality: devotion to Jesus our Divine Master, to Mary, Queen of Apostles, and to St. Paul the Apostle.

Blessed James Alberione's Marian Spirituality

"SPIRITUALITY" HAS TWO MEANINGS: the way a particular person lives out his or her relationship with God, and a spiritual teaching to share with others. In both senses Alberione's spirituality is thoroughly Marian. He always had a strong personal devotion to Mary, and he developed a unique approach to Mary that springs from his apostolic charism.

From his roots, Alberione imbibed a loving devotion to Mary. Shortly after his birth, his mother dedicated him to the Blessed Virgin at the nearby shrine of Our Lady of the Flowers. As James grew, his mother often brought him to visit the shrine. He "breathed in" this atmosphere of popular Marian piety. As a priest, Alberione often prayed at various Marian shrines throughout Piedmont, counting on Mary's help to overcome difficulties. He developed a vital, deeply personal relationship with Mary.

When Blessed Alberione wanted to sum up his approach to spirituality, he wrote: "The Pauline Family strives to live fully the

Gospel of Jesus Christ, Way, Truth, and Life, in the spirit of St. Paul, under the gaze of the Queen of Apostles" (*Abundantes*, n. 93). The key phrase, "under the gaze" of Mary, indicates that she always watches over us like a loving mother. For Alberione, Marian devotion did not consist of particular devotional practices. Although he daily prayed the Rosary and wrote a number of Marian prayers, his Marian spirituality meant living in a Marian "climate." He wanted *devotion*, not devotions; he wanted to live in a profoundly Marian way.

Precisely because it's not a method tied to particular practices, Alberione's Marian spirituality can be difficult to pin down. The key thought quoted above suggests it concerns living in Mary's maternal presence. To live "under Mary's gaze" expresses the essence of his Marian spirituality. For Alberione, Mary is present in the life of each Christian through every stage, from birth to death, and because presence implies relationship, living in Mary's presence means developing a personal relationship with her.

Queen of the Apostles

OF ALL MARY'S TITLES, Alberione preferred "Queen of the Apostles." He once explained how this devotion to Mary as Queen of Apostles began in his young institute:

> On December 8, 1919, the feast of the Immaculate Conception, the clerics and aspirants came to me to ask under what title we would invoke Mary and what would be our devotion, e.g., Help of Christians, Mother of Divine Grace, Mother of Good Counsel, etc. I had already given thought and prayer to this and so my answer was: "Invoke Mary under the title Queen of Apostles; first, for the sanctification of Apostles; second, that those who were helping the Apostles would receive their reward; and third, that both Apostles and faithful would be all together in heaven." (*Sermons on the Queen of Apostles*, 234)

Throughout his life, Alberione developed that original inspiration. His Marian spirituality has two goals: personal holiness and apostolic mission. Both of these aspects lead us to Jesus Christ.

Marian Devotion Centered on Jesus Christ

ALBERIONE'S MARIAN devotion ties in with his emphasis on the central place of Jesus Christ in the spiritual life. Between World War II and Vatican II, Marian devotion in the twentieth century reached its height. Some proponents of popular devotion at the time seemed to emphasize Mary more than Jesus, but not Alberione. He always saw Mary in relation to Christ. Although his major work took place before Vatican II, in many ways he anticipated certain themes of the Council. The *Dogmatic Constitution on the Church*, for example, stated this about Marian devotion: "In no way does it impede, but rather does it foster the immediate union of the faithful with Christ" (n. 60). The Council wanted to correct some of the excesses and emphasize that Marian devotion leads us to Jesus Christ. Alberione was already doing this. His Marian spirituality concerns a profound devotion that goes to the basis of the Christian life.

For Blessed Alberione, Jesus is the center of everything. His fundamental concern was that we should grow in the image of Jesus the Divine Master, our Way, Truth, and Life. We are grafted in Christ through Baptism, and need to grow continually in this life "until Christ is formed in you" (Gal 4:19). This was Alberione's fundamental goal of life.

And according to him, this is precisely where Mary comes in. The main goal of our life is that Christ be formed in us to the point where we can say: "It is no longer I who live, but Christ living in me" (Gal 2:20), and Mary plays a key role in this process. Just as she formed Jesus in her womb, bringing the Word Incarnate into the world, so she forms Jesus in us. Alberione wrote:

> As Mary carried Jesus in her womb from the moment of the angel's words, so she bore the Church in her heart from the moment she heard her Son's words: "Woman, behold your son." She carried the child Jesus in her arms; she carried the newborn Church in her arms. (*Spiritual Exercises* from 1960, page 514)

Alberione compares this to a new Incarnation of Christ: through Mary, we are transformed into Jesus.

This change affects our whole being. Alberione saw the three aspects of Jesus—Way, Truth, and Life—as corresponding to the threefold aspect of the human person—mind, will, and heart. In a shorthand way, he referred to this approach as the devotion to Jesus, the Divine Master. For Alberione, "master" does not signify a lord, much less an overseer or a taskmaster, but primarily a teacher. Jesus is a Master Teacher who has the heart of a shepherd.

Corresponding to this image, he constantly referred to Mary as our "Mother, Teacher, and Queen." As Mother, Mary forms the life of Jesus in us; as Teacher, she, the first disciple of Jesus, also instructs us on how to be disciples; and as Queen, she leads us on the way to her Son. She is a Queen who does not dominate but who serves.

The teaching of Pope Leo XIII influenced Alberione's thought in this regard. As a seminarian and a young priest, Alberione read Leo's encyclical *Tametsi Futura*, which planted the seeds of devotion to Jesus Master in his mind. Similarly, he found inspiration for devotion to Mary, Queen of Apostles, in Leo's encyclical, *Adiutricem Populi*. The Pope wrote of Mary:

> With wonderful care she nurtured the first Christians by her holy example, her authoritative counsel, her sweet consolation, her fruitful prayers. She was in very truth the Mother of the Church, the Teacher and Queen of the Apostles, to whom, besides, she confided no small part of the divine mysteries which she kept in her heart.

Alberione meditated on these words, and these three titles—"Mother, Teacher, and Queen"—became a favorite theme for him and a constant refrain in the Marian prayers he wrote.

Besides Pope Leo XIII, Alberione also drew on other sources in developing his devotion to Mary, Queen of Apostles. These included the thought of St. Vincent Pallotti, founder of the Pallotines, who had developed an apostolic Marian spirituality. Alberione also looked into the writings of the Fathers of the Church about Mary, as Sr. Luigina Borrano, FSP, testified: "In 1937, Fr. Alberione sent me to the superior of the Pallotine Fathers, to ask if they possessed writings on the theological and patristic foundations for devotion to Mary, 'Queen of Apostles.'"

Mary and Evangelization

ABOVE ALL ELSE, Alberione saw Mary as an Apostle, because she gave Jesus to the world. As his mother, she had a unique vocation in giving Jesus to us through his physical birth. No one else could do that. But on the spiritual level, every baptized Christian can and must bring Jesus to the world today. This is what evangelization means. So we look to Mary as our model in bringing the Good News to everyone. Using a play on words that relates to the communications mission he had at heart, Alberione liked to say that Mary "published" Jesus. As he put it in a prayer to Mary, "You gave the world the book to read, the Eternal Word." He also wrote:

> Publishers possess the word. They multiply it and distribute it clothed in paper, type, and ink. On the human level, they have the mission that Mary had on the divine level. She was the Mother of the divine Word. She contained the invisible God and made him visible and accessible to us by presenting him in human flesh. (*CISP*, 1971, p. 599)

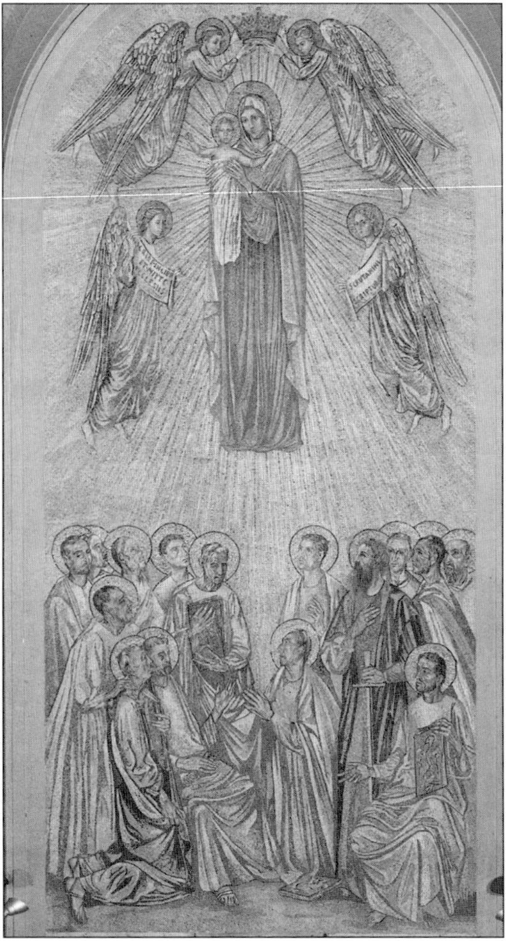

In the Church, Mary still carries out this maternal role in regard to those whom God calls in every age to continue his apostolic mission.

The Image of Mary, Queen of Apostles

BEING A MAN of the media, Alberione understood the power of image and commissioned a painting and a statue to represent devotion to Mary as Queen of Apostles. In those images Mary does not hold the child Jesus to herself, as many artists depict her. Instead, she holds Jesus out as if offering him to the world. This represents her key role of giving Jesus to humanity—to every person—and every other apostle does the same thing in different ways. Alberione once commented:

> One time I heard this odd statement: "In the image of the Queen of Apostles there is nothing referring to the apostolate." But isn't Mary depicted giving Jesus? What else is the apostolate but the giving of Jesus? You do not distribute bread; you distribute truth, and by this you give Jesus to the world. (Unpublished sermons of

Blessed James Alberione on the Queen of Apostles, SSP Archives, p. 178)

The Queen of Apostles Basilica

ALBERIONE CROWNED his Marian legacy when he built the Queen of Apostles Basilica, located at 75 Via Antonino Pio, Rome. He did this after World War II to fulfill a promise he had made to the Blessed Mother, in gratitude that all the members of his religious institutes survived the war.

The art and architecture of the basilica express a key aspect of Alberione's Marian spirituality: Mary as the Mother of all humanity. He had gleaned this idea from Pope Leo XIII's encyclical, along with the ideas that Mary is the Queen of Apostles, the Mother of Unity, and the exemplar and sustainer of universal prayer. The great cupola of the basilica shows Mary as the Mother of all people. She spreads out her mantle as if to embrace the whole world, to protect and help all peoples. A lovely mosaic image of Mary as Queen of Apostles graces the wall above the altar. The subcrypt of the church has other beautiful mosaics that express concepts from a meditative prayer Alberione wrote entitled "The Way of Humanity." In the introduction to this prayer, Blessed Alberione highlights Mary's role:

> Everything comes from God-beginning, to return to God-end: for his glory and the happiness of all people. Mary guides us to the sure way, which is Christ, in the Church founded by him. In Christ Way, Truth, and Life, we are adopted and made heirs, sons and daughters of God. Through the invisible Christ, in the visible Church, humanity possesses temporal and eternal good. All of us are awaited in the home of the heavenly Father; through Mary everyone can find Christ the Way. May everyone point out this way in the spirit of charity and apostolate.

EDITOR'S NOTE

The quotations in this volume are taken from the spoken and written texts that Blessed James Alberione gave to the Pauline Family. Most of them have been published only for internal use in the institutes he founded. The specific source of each quotation has not been included in this volume so as to not weigh it down with excessive footnotes and references.

Chapter 1

MARY GIVES JESUS TO US

"O Mary,
I contemplate the great moment
of the Incarnation of the Word,
when you became the Mother of God.
At that moment you also became
the Mother of humanity and
the Queen of saints,
especially of the Apostles...."

THE FIVE CHAPTERS OF THIS BOOK correspond to the five points of a chaplet Blessed Alberione wrote to honor Mary, Queen of Apostles. In the first point he contemplates Mary receiving God's message from the angel Gabriel. From the moment she accepted God's invitation to become the Mother of his Son, Mary stepped into history as the woman who gives us Jesus. For Alberione, this is the basis for Marian devotion; her role is to give birth to and form Jesus in us.

Mary gave birth to the Son of God while remaining a virgin because she entrusted herself totally to God. Her virginity does not devalue God's gift of marriage and sexuality, but is a sign that points to the divinity of Jesus, whose only Father is God. In giving us Jesus, Mary became the spiritual Mother of all humanity. Her joyful readiness to fulfill God's will was so great that her faith can be compared to Abraham's. In fact, Pope John Paul II has said that "Mary's faith at the Annunciation inaugurates the New Covenant" (*Redemptoris Mater*, n. 14). The opening thought from Alberione picks up this theme, which leads into the reflections on Mary as the way to reach Jesus.

Mary: Dawn of the New Covenant

When the fullness of time at last
    arrives,
Mary comes into the world
as the dawn of the New Covenant
and in the full splendor
of her immaculate conception.

Christ My Life

*C*hrist is my life,
and the way to reach him
is Mary.

Mary and the Plan of God

*C*onsider yourselves as Mary.
Then you will understand
the plan of God.
Mary fulfilled it perfectly,
because she was docile,
because she was humble.
"I am the handmaid of the Lord" (Lk 1:38).

Mary's Work

*P*rogress in virtue and merits...
requires a continual flow of graces.
It means replacing human thoughts with
Christian principles and reasoning.
It means being able to say with truth:
"I live now not with my own life
but with the life of Christ who lives in
 me" (Gal 2:20).
All this is the work of Mary.
She formed Jesus Christ,
considered as a physical human being;
she received then the vocation
and the grace to form Jesus Christ,
considered as the Mystical Body.

Mary: the Way to Jesus

It is necessary that our devotions
be always more grafted onto Jesus
 Master,
the Queen of Apostles, and St. Paul,
 Apostle.
Jesus Christ is the Master;
he is the Apostle of the Father.
We are to know him always better.
The journey to be made is unending:
"Be perfect just as your
heavenly Father is perfect" (Mt 5:48).
Who will reach such a height?
Who will reach the point of identifying
her or himself with Christ?
The way to reach this union is Mary.
One who is more devoted to Mary

will unite him or herself more intimately
   to Jesus Christ.
Let there be simple and fervent
devotion to Mary.

Mary's Faith

*M*ary's faith was truly exceptional.
She believed the angel,
believed in the marvelous mystery
of the Incarnation.
Elizabeth said to her,
"Blessed are you because you believed."

Mary Radiates Jesus Christ

*E*very apostolate is a radiating of Jesus Christ;
it is to give something,
if we can use the expression,
of Jesus Christ....
Mary gave us the whole Christ, Way, Truth, and Life.
She is the Apostle empowered by God.

Mary Gives Birth to Jesus in Us

The task of the Virgin Mother
is to gradually bring about
the birth of Jesus
and to form Jesus
in all those who should conform
to the image of her Son.

The Father's Beloved Son

Mary,
grant that the human race
will heed the invitation
of the heavenly Father:
"This is my beloved Son
in whom I am well pleased.
Listen to him!"

Seek Mary's Help

The Pauline Family has the mission
of making Jesus Christ known, imitated,
and lived as the Master.
It will carry out this privileged mission
in a holy manner by making Mary,
> Teacher,

known, loved, and invoked.
"She gave the world Jesus Master,
who is the blessed fruit of her womb."
Pauline teaching will be immensely more
> effective

if it is inspired, guided, and comforted by
> Mary:

"With her help you will not grow tired."
No one would want to deprive
him or herself of such a great help.

Pauline discipleship is to be wholly
 grafted onto Mary,
who will form Jesus Christ in everyone.
This means becoming Christians,
 apostles, saints.

The Easy Way

*D*evotion to Mary
is for all those who want
to attain [life in] Jesus Christ
more quickly, easily, and surely.

To Find Jesus, Go to Mary

When the shepherds and the magi
went to Bethlehem,
they found Jesus in Mary's arms.
Mary showed him [to them] and then
presented him in the Temple,
where Simeon and Anna recognized him.
Mary enables us to know Jesus
according to the time,
the situation, and the tasks [that we face].

Mary Gives Jesus

*L*ike a branch that always bears fruit
and offers it to humanity,
Mary gives Jesus—
suffering, glorious, Eucharistic,
the Way, the Truth, and the Life
of all people.
She is the Apostle of Jesus, not only
in word but in mind, will, and heart.
Rather than with ink, she wrote Jesus—
that is, formed him in herself—
by the power of the Holy Spirit....
In giving Jesus,
she gave us the holy Gospel in him.
In giving Jesus,
she presented every perfection in him.
In giving Jesus,
she gave us the redemption, the
   Eucharist, Life....

Mary Continues to Give Jesus to the World

Why did God make Mary Mother of God
and of the Church? So that she would be
the Queen of the Apostles and the true
   Apostle.
Hence, her very dignity as Mother of
   God
is in relation to her office as Apostle—
to give Jesus to the world,
to give him as the God-man,
and to give [him to] the Church
until the consummation of time,
because today Christ is the Church.
To listen to the Church is to listen to
   Jesus Christ.
Mary is the Apostle.

Relative to us she is Queen because she calls us
to participate in her apostolate,
because she is greater than all apostles,
and because she gathers and instructs all apostles.
To them she gives graces and prepares the reward of glory.

Mary Helps Us to Follow God's Will

*T*he first and principal
homage to Mary
consists in the effort to
do the will of her divine Son;
may every prayer and wish
offered to her be guided by that intention.
Our good Mother Mary,
who is full of grace
and is mediatrix of all grace,
listens to us if this is the principal
and constant request we make of her....
As a wise and loving Mother,
Mary helps us fulfill the will of God.

CHAPTER 2

MARY IS THE MOTHER OF ALL HUMANITY

*"O Mary,
I contemplate the scene on Calvary,
when from the cross
Jesus proclaimed you Mother
of St. John the Apostle,
and in him Mother of all humanity,
especially of the Apostles...."*

IN SOME SURPRISING WAYS, Alberione's emphasis on Mary as the Mother of all humanity anticipated Pope John Paul II's approach to Mary, which hinges on respect for freedom and the human person. The opening thought in this chapter stresses Mary's freedom and God's respect for it. Her free consent at the Annunciation paved the way for her second "yes" on Calvary. As she stood by the cross, her role as the Mother of all humanity took on a new aspect because of the unique way she cooperated in the redeeming work of her Son, Jesus.

This chapter ushers us from contemplating Mary in the mystery of Christ to contemplating her in the mystery of the Church. As Mother of the Church, Mary is Mother of all humanity, but because a mother is always a mother of a unique person, Mary is the Mother of humanity not just in a general way but of each one of us in particular. So we can turn to her with complete confidence and trust. Jesus himself encouraged us to do this by entrusting the beloved disciple to Mary's care. In John's Gospel, the beloved disciple goes unnamed because he is meant to represent every believer. Like him, Jesus asks us to welcome Mary into our lives.

Allow God to Enter Your Heart

*O*n Mary depended the permission—
the word is correct—
for Jesus to come into the world
and to fulfill the mission
entrusted to him by the Father.
The Father, the Son, and the Holy Spirit
respected her freedom.
We too are free to permit God
to enter our hearts!
Mary was astonished;
she asked for an explanation,
and then pronounced her *fiat:*
"Let what you have said be done to me"
   (Lk 1:38).

Mary's Sufferings

Before Mary's own eyes,
Jesus was treated cruelly,
stripped of his clothes, and nailed to the cross.
St. John the Evangelist says:
"Standing by the cross of Jesus
were his mother, and his mother's sister,
Mary the wife of Clopas, and Mary Magdalene" (Jn 19:25)....
Mary offered her Son; she offered herself.
There were two altars on Calvary:
the cross for her Son;
the heart pierced by a sharp sword for Mary.

Mary on Calvary

O Mary...remember
that painful and solemn moment
in which the dying Jesus
from the cross gave you
John as your son,
and in him all humanity and
especially all the Apostles.
In virtue of your unspeakable sufferings
and those of your divine Son,
through the love of your motherly heart,
　Mary,
increase the number of apostles,
missionaries, priests, religious, and laity.

*Mother of Humanity**

*W*e turn to you, O Mary,
to your beautiful throne,
and considering the present and the future,
we pray:
O Queen,
turn your merciful eyes upon us;
like Esther, you have found favor with
    the King.
Your universal solicitude
as the "Mother of humanity"
and your role as mediatrix of grace
fill us with confidence
in presenting these petitions
for our needs and for those of the
    Church and of humanity.

---

* Blessed Alberione composed this prayer for the dedication of the Queen of Apostles Basilica in Rome.

Two Great Women

*E*ve, the first woman,
was the mother of the living;
Mary, the second woman,
is the Mother of the redeemed.
Redemption began
with Mary's "yes"!
"Behold the handmaid of the Lord;
may it be done unto me
according to your word."
...We have two women,
two great women,
at the head of humanity:
Eve...and Mary....
Mary is the great Woman,
as Jesus called her:
"Woman, behold your son!"

Confide in Mary Because She Cares About You

One of the first episodes in the Divine Master's public life is the wedding feast at Cana. Jesus and his disciples were invited, and so was Mary, Jesus' Mother. In this narrative we see Mary's attentiveness to the needs of others. She is at the wedding, but she is not so much concerned about the external feast as she is eager to see that all proceeds smoothly, that the holy joy is not disturbed. She is anxious to spare the bridal couple embarrassment...due to the lack of wine—so important at a wedding feast. She is the first to notice it: "They have no wine" (Jn 2:3). Immediately, she thinks of a remedy and intervenes with prayer.

Mary has boundless care and solicitude for each of her children. Her prayer is very brief but humble, accompanied by great and most powerful faith. She is the Mother of Jesus. This is the main reason for her power....

Mary has wisdom to know our necessities, goodness which is moved by our miseries, and power to intercede for us and come to our assistance. This is why we should confide in this Mother.

Her eyes are turned toward all her children, the just and the sinners, in order to discern our spiritual and material needs, difficulties, and dangers. She knows them all. Moreover, she is more sensitive and compassionate than any earthly mother, even the best. She is the Mother of Mercy.

Mother of Divine Grace

*I*n the Salve Regina,
the Church has us greet Mary as life;
indeed, in the litanies,
as Mother of Divine Grace.
It is not she who produced grace,
but it is her role to communicate it.
She is Mother because
Jesus-Life passed through her.

Mary, the Way of God

*T*he redemption came through Mary,
and this is the road
marked out by God.
We must follow it as did God.
He willed and wills
to give us everything through Mary.

All Good Comes Through Mary

The Church is entrusted to Mary.
In creation, in redemption,
in the distribution of graces and in the
    order of glory,
Mary occupies a preeminent place.
She gives Jesus Christ to the world
and to every person.
All good things
have passed through Mary.
From Mary comes life.
She is our Mother.

Mary Is Our Spiritual Mother

At Nazareth Mary conceived us.
Our spiritual conception occurred
in the mystery of the Incarnation.
Without the Incarnation
we would still be buried in the death of sin.
Now God has worked the Incarnation
through Mary, and willed
that her cooperation
be free, conscious, and necessary.
Her *fiat* was an act of consent
for our supernatural conception
and for her motherhood in our regard.

Holy Desires

Mary is the woman Apostle par
excellence,
because she is the model
of the greatest interior life.
She performed this apostolate
in the most perfect manner.
She is also the Apostle of holy desires,
because she, more than anyone else,
desired that the redemption be fulfilled.

Mary Our Hope

Mary is the hope of sinners,
of the exiled, of prisoners.
She is the consoler of the afflicted.

Jesus' Way, Our Way

To carry out our redemption
the Son of God came through Mary.
To every person the Lord applies
salvation and sanctification,
life and the increase of life through Mary.
Jesus Christ came to us through Mary....
He is the Way, even in the Incarnation.
The way marked out for us is to be
 followed.

Chapter 3

MARY, QUEEN OF APOSTLES

*"O Mary,
I contemplate the days in the Cenacle
when you were Teacher and Queen of the
    Apostles,
invoking and receiving
the Holy Spirit and his gifts...."*

AT THE ANNUNCIATION, the Holy Spirit overshadowed Mary in a personal way, and she became the Mother of God. At Pentecost, the Holy Spirit overshadowed Mary and the Apostles, and confirmed her as Mother of the Church. Mary opened herself so entirely to the Holy Spirit that she was completely attuned to "what the Spirit is saying to the churches" (Rev 2:7). This is why Alberione chose the scene of Mary among the Apostles to visually express her role as Queen of the Apostles.

She gave the Apostles the gift of her motherly care, her prayer, her example. Mary's role, however, was not to be part of the hierarchy of the Church (the Petrine dimension), but to be the model of holiness and prayer (the Marian dimension). Ultimately, the Church is all about leading people to salvation. That is why we can affirm that "the 'Marian' dimension of the Church precedes the 'Petrine'" (*Catechism of the Catholic Church*, n. 773). In other words, holiness surpasses everything.

Mary, Queen of Every Family

The Blessed Mother can be addressed
with various titles—Immaculate,
Queen of Martyrs, Queen of Virgins—
but from you she expects the title
Queen of Apostles, and she expects
devotion in conformity with this title.
Know the Queen of Apostles....
When all is done for the Queen,
progress and a good spirit are
    immediately seen.
Make Mary Queen of every house.
She will govern well,
just as she did in the house of Nazareth.

The First Devotion

The first devotion we find in the Church
is devotion to the Queen of Apostles,
as expressed in the Cenacle. It lessened a bit
and became obscure with the passing
of the centuries. You have the sweet mission
of gathering the faithful around
Mary, Queen of the Apostles.
You are to reawaken this devotion.
You are to fulfill this most delightful
mission in the Church. It means reawakening
all apostolates and arousing vocations.
Let us return to the sources. At the sources
we find Mary, Queen of the Apostles.

If it was so at the beginning of the Church,
there is nothing more certain than to draw
from the ancient Faith. The water is purer
when it is taken from its source.

Why We Honor Mary

*T*he Apostle par excellence is Jesus.
Mary is the Apostle not in the same way
Jesus is, but still in a manner
immensely greater than all other apostles.
The first Apostles and apostles of all times
merit this name inasmuch as
they share the apostolate of Jesus and Mary.
Whoever makes himself more similar to
   Mary
participates in Mary's apostolate.
This is your vocation:
to participate in Mary's apostolate.
All the privileges of Mary most holy
were directed toward rendering her
Mother of God and Queen of the
   Apostles.

For this reason we honor her as
>   Immaculate, assumed,
but above all as Queen of the Apostles,
because we sum up all her privileges in
>   this title.

The Face of an Apostle

An apostle is one who bears God
in her own soul and radiates God
to those around her.
The apostle is a saint who accumulates treasures,
and communicates the overflow to others.
This is a heart that loves God and souls
so intensely that it can no longer
confine within itself what it feels and thinks.
Apostles are ostensoriums that hold Jesus Christ
and shed indescribable light all around.
They are vessels of election who overflow
because they are too full,
and whose fullness all can enjoy.

They are temples of the most Holy
Trinity,
who is supremely active;
they exude God from all their pores—
with words, actions, prayers, gestures,
and attitudes....
Now, with this picture, examine the faces
of persons near and far and see if you
recognize
the apostle in them. In the greatest
measure,
with incomparable resemblance,
this is Mary's face.

Mary, Our Hope

*M*ary is Queen of the Apostles
because she is the hope
of all those called to do good
in the immense and
fertile apostolate of the Church.

Mary and the Church

*M*ary brought and brings
to the Church
the greatest fruit of salvation
and always new outpourings
of the Holy Spirit.

Mother of the Divine Word

*E*ditors possess the word, multiply it,
and diffuse it clothed in paper, words,
    and ink.
On a human plane they have the mission
that Mary had in the divine plan
as Mother of the Divine Word.
She won the favor
of the invisible God
and rendered him visible and
accessible to humanity,
presenting him in human flesh.

Why Mary Is Queen of the Apostles

*M*ary is the Queen of the Apostles for
> three reasons.
She possesses and fulfills everything
that all apostles, taken together,
possess and fulfill
now and in the future.
In addition, she possesses and
fulfills an apostolate
which exceeds and surpasses
all other apostolates put together.
Further, hers is the duty of forming,
> guiding,
supporting, and giving fruit and
reward to all apostles.
From the first instant of the Incarnation,
through Jesus Christ, in the womb of
> Mary,

with Mary and through Mary,
the glorification and praise of God
began that forms the first and perfect
 apostolate.
And the redemption,
the second apostolate, also began.
A deeper knowledge of Mary
and her title of Apostle,
of Mother, Teacher, and Queen of the
 Apostles,
is being developed.

Think and Love Like Jesus and Mary

Yes, hold it for certain
that we cannot be truly devoted to Mary
unless we thirst for souls as Jesus.
We will not resemble either Jesus the Apostle,
or Mary the Apostle,
because only imitators are children
of Mary and united to Jesus.
If we do not possess
the mind and heart of Jesus and Mary,
how can we live a life
of union with Jesus and Mary?
To all those who love God, Jesus recalls:
"The second [commandment]
resembles [the first]:
You must love your neighbor..." (Mt 23:38–39).

Goals of Marian Devotion

Devotion to Mary,
which is a part of the Pauline spirit,
has two ends for us:
our religious sanctification
and the pastoral apostolate,
that is, reaching souls.
"To Jesus through Mary."
Write well of Mary
because she is the way to go to Jesus,
the easiest way.

Stay with Mary

*M*ary is the Queen of Apostles.
If we are to perform the apostolate,
let us stay with Mary....
Mary helps in every apostolate;
she enlightens and will reward.

Walking with Mary

*F*ollowing the Apostles,
all the announcers of the Gospel,
the preachers of the divine Word,
set out from the feet of Mary;
they begin with the name of Mary.

Mary's Unique Role

The Queen of Apostles—of her we are
 to believe:
that she was the Mother of the Apostle of
 the Father, the Divine Word;
that she became Mother, Teacher, and
 Queen
of every apostle at the birth of Jesus,
 their head;
that she was proclaimed such by Jesus on
 the cross;
that she showed herself to be such
with the Apostles, especially at Pentecost;
that she was always the inspirer and
protectress of every apostolate—
of the word and of the pen—
and the one who formed apostles
of every place and time.

Entrust Everything to Mary

We honor Mary under the title of
Mother and Teacher,
but above all under the title of Queen.
To her we entrust all vocations and
all the apostolate, so that she may be
the inspirer, protecting all those
who consecrate themselves to her.
We are to offer all that is in us to Mary
so that all will be offered to Jesus.

Queen of Pentecost

At Pentecost, in fact,
we find Mary, Mother of the Church
and Queen of the Apostles;
Mother, Queen, and Teacher
of all peoples in every age.
Queen of heaven and of earth,
distributor of all graces.

Mary and the Holy Spirit

O Mary, obtain the Holy Spirit
for those persons committed to the
  spread of the Gospel.
May they experience a renewal of
  Pentecost.
Give us the gift of the word:
oral, written, photographed, transmitted,
according to the will of God.

Mary Is the Apostle

*M*ary was created for the apostolate
to give Jesus Christ to the world:
he who is the Way, the Truth, and the
 Life;
he who is Teacher, Priest, and Victim—
 God!
Jesus is the Apostle:
"We have our high priest and Apostle,
Jesus Christ" (Heb 3:1).
Mary is the Apostle with Christ,
in dependence on Christ,
sharing in the apostolate with Christ.

Mary at the Heart of Mission

*B*y nature Mary is essentially an apostle.
She came to give Jesus,
to bring life to souls,
to be mediatrix and distributrix of grace....
Jesus is the Apostle for this reason:
"I have come so that they may have life"
  (Jn 10:10).
Mary came to bring us the Life—Christ.
She is an apostle in the prophecies,
in life, and in heaven!
To establish Marian devotion
is to place the Virgin
at the very heart of her apostolate
toward humanity and individuals,
toward secular society and the Church,
for the kingdom of God and his glory.

Chapter 4

MARY OUR TEACHER

*"O Mary,
I contemplate the moment
in which the Lord's all-powerful love
raised you from death
and assumed you into heaven.
There the most Holy Trinity
crowned you Queen of heaven and of
earth...."*

ALBERIONE STRESSED WHAT HE CALLED "the sanctification of the mind"—that is, soaking one's mind in the truths of the Gospel, just like a desert soaks up rain. In this way, we can think more and more like Jesus, as St. Paul said: "Let the same mind be in you that was in Christ Jesus" (Phil 2:5). Blessed James often spoke of going to the "school" of Jesus. In that school,

Mary is our best Teacher because of her closeness to him.

It is appropriate to think of Mary as our Teacher in light of her Assumption and glorification. From heaven, she intercedes for us and obtains many graces to guide us on our way through life. Her Queenship is one of service, as Pope John Paul II has said: "The glory of serving does not cease to be her royal exaltation: assumed into heaven, she does not cease her saving service" (*Redemptoris Mater*, n. 41). While all Christian service builds up the Church, that of teaching is especially noble since it opens our minds to the light of God's truth.

Jesus, the One Teacher

*J*esus is our one and only Teacher.
Mary is our Teacher
in association with, in dependence on,
and in relation to Jesus Christ.

Mary Watches Over Apostles of All Times

The most holy Virgin showed herself
as Queen of the Apostles
especially after her Assumption into
    heaven.
It was then that she began a new phase
of her apostolic mission. From then on
she raised up every kind of apostle:
apostles of action and of word,
of example and of the pen,
of charity and of truth.
All times and all needs, corporal and
    spiritual,
had to have their apostles.
Mary received from God the sublime
    mission
of calling and forming apostles

of all times and for every field.
Mary is the protecting angel of the
    missions...
She wants all those who dedicate
    themselves
to the apostolate close to her in heaven.

Teacher of Jesus

Various authors list the duties of Mary toward her son. She dressed him with normal clothes; she nourished him with her milk and with bread, the fruit of her labors; she carried him in her arms; with Joseph she saved him, going into exile in Egypt, and she brought him back into Galilee; she guided his first steps; she taught him prayers from Sacred Scripture; she defended him from natural dangers; she taught him to speak with men; she prepared him for immolation; she buried his body....

Everything—from the Annunciation, which was to be fulfilled according to the prophecies, and the preparation of the Master, the Victim and the Priest for humanity—Mary understood, enlightened by the Holy Spirit. She understood the plans of God and cooperated with her whole mind and activity at

Bethlehem, at the Presentation in the Temple, during the hidden life, the public life, and the passion....

Now Mary, assumed into heaven, is in eternal beatitude, with her whole being focused on the divine Essence. She sees God and, in God, the mysteries of grace, all creatures, and each one of us in particular. She is there as universal mediatrix, and also has the task of distributing wisdom to whomever she wills and as much as she wills.

Teacher of the Apostles

Before dying, Jesus said to John, "There is your Mother." He said it because from that moment on a new and most important task was to begin for Mary, that is, the task of becoming spiritual Mother of all humanity.

After the crucifixion of Jesus, the apostolic college underwent a tremendous crisis. A person was needed who enjoyed the trust of the Apostles, and who would gather them together and instruct them. Such a person was Mary. She gathered them together in the Cenacle and prepared them to receive the Holy Spirit. Not only this, but she was also their Teacher during that whole period of waiting. She instructed them especially about a mystery they had not known—the mystery of the Incarnation. She also told them about many other details in Jesus' private life which she alone knew.

Teacher of All Christians

*M*ary is primarily Mother and Teacher
   of faith,
because what she did for the Apostles
during the stormy period
following the death of Jesus,
she still does on all those occasions
in Christian history when the faith
is seriously threatened.
Jesus Christ, by constituting her our
   Mother,
willed to entrust this mission to her
   especially.
In each new crisis the Church goes
   through,
Mary opposes with her defense,
revealing herself to all people
especially as Teacher of truth and faith.

Mary Receives Us into the School of Jesus

*R*eceive me, O Mary,
Mother, Teacher, and Queen,
among those whom you love, nourish,
sanctify, and guide
in the school of Jesus Christ,
the Divine Master.

Mary, Disciple of Jesus

Mary was first a disciple,
then a teacher. She was a disciple—
the most diligent and intelligent of all
    creatures.
She, who was furnished
with the most sublime mind,
exempt from original sin,
from error and distractions,
always remained under the action of the
    Sun of light:
"The Word was the true light
that enlightens all men" (Jn 1:9).
In particular, she was the pupil
first of the Incarnation,
then during the private life of Jesus,
and afterward during his public life.

Mary Treasured Jesus' Words

Disciple during Jesus' private life.

By intimately living together with Jesus for thirty years, Mary learned all the spirit of the New Testament, which Jesus first lived in himself, in his sanctity—he "began to act, awaiting the hour of teaching."

The Annunciation was a profound revelation. A world of things is to be learned from this event. The same is true of the visit to St. Elizabeth, the Nativity, the Presentation in the Temple, and the hidden life in Nazareth....

Mary saw, remembered, meditated. St. Luke notes two times: "As for Mary, she treasured all these things and pondered them in her heart" (Lk 2:19, 51).

Together with Jesus, Mary also grew spiritually, and her soul became enriched and fortified in virtue. The heavenly Father must have observed this with joy, been delighted, and turned his pleased gaze on Mary also.

Disciple during Jesus' public life.

*T*he Gospels give sufficient indication to convince us that Mary followed Jesus for a great part of his public life...

Two observations are certainly to be made:
1. Mary was the intelligent, enthusiastic disciple who welcomed the divine message of Jesus Christ and lived it in her daily life, her effort being unique among believers.
2. She was the most faithful and exact interpreter of Jesus' teachings, even those that were the highest and most sublime. She treasured his words and fully absorbed them into her heart and soul.

Mary followed Jesus sometimes near at hand, sometimes from afar.... She prayed for the fulfillment of her Son's mission.

Mary, Our Guide to Jesus

No one knew Christ
so well and profoundly
as Mary did.
No one is a better guide and teacher
to make us know Christ than Mary.

Mary, God's Masterpiece

When God finds a soul as humble
and docile to his will as was Mary most
   holy,
he uses it to fulfill his plans
of charity and wisdom.
But it must be as docile
as a brush in the hands of an artist!...
This is how God found Mary and Joseph,
as well as the Apostles.

Our Mother, Teacher, and Queen

*O*ur devotion toward Jesus,
the Divine Master, will be perfected
if it is prepared for and preceded by
devotion to Mary, Teacher.
Leo XIII in the Encyclical,
Adiutricem Populi Christiani, wrote:
"In all truth Mary must be considered
Mother of the Church,
Teacher, and Queen of the Apostles,
to whom she imparted even those divine
 teachings
which she preserved in her heart."
Therefore, Mary is Teacher.
If it is said, "To Jesus through Mary,"
worthy also will be the phrase:
"To Jesus Master through Mary Teacher."
First she was pupil, then teacher,
then mother and guardian of teachers.

Teacher in the Church

*M*ary became the most humble
and ardent Teacher
of the evangelical message.
She would have liked to diffuse it
throughout the world and
share it with all people
to bring them salvation and happiness.

Mary Shows Us the Way

Mary, model of every disciple of Jesus,
obtain for us your docility.
Drive away from us pride, prejudice,
stubbornness, and the passions
which harden the heart and darken the mind.
Mary, Mother of the Master
and yet his disciple,
guide me on your path.

Imitate Mary

We are to choose Mary as Teacher....
Invoke her as a Teacher who is wise,
holy, and full of grace.
We are to ask her for her spirit
and her love for souls.
We are to imitate her in patient charity.
The teacher...should consecrate
his or her students and entrust them
to Mary, the Teacher.

Magnificat!

Our life
must be a Magnificat.
We must magnify the Lord
as the Blessed Mother did.

CHAPTER 5

MARY HELPS US TO PRAY

*"O Mary,
Queen of the Church and of the universe,
I contemplate you in heavenly glory
where you exercise your mercy
as mediatrix and distributor of all graces...."*

WHILE THE CONCEPT OF QUEENSHIP might seem outdated to many people today, it can be thought of in terms of leadership and service. Scripture says that the whole people of God have a share in God's kingdom: "If we endure, we will also reign with him" (2 Tim 2:12). Mary's Queenship is a special sharing in the royal condition of all those who live with God. As Queen, Mary helps us to pray. For Alberione, devotion to Mary comprises not only prayer but knowledge and imitation, as the opening thought of this chapter points out.

Alberione often used the terms "mediatrix" and "dispenser (or distributor) of graces," which were common in his day. However, since Vatican II the Church's language about Mary's intercessory role has shifted. Official documents have avoided the term "mediatrix" in order to avoid confusion about Mary's role in relation to Christ. He alone is our redeemer and our sole mediator with the Father. Mary's role always remains subordinate to that of Jesus. John Paul II uses the term "maternal mediation" to express Mary's role, and he developed this concept at length in his encyclical, *Mother of the Redeemer*. Mary's maternal mediation expresses the reality that her role is unique precisely because she is the Mother of God.

Surrender to God

Why does Mary have so much glory?
Mary corresponded perfectly
to her mission, to her vocation,
and to the plans of God.
What a great secret of merit and glory!
We too have a special vocation,
and God bound us with so many
chains of graces that we are obliged
to surrender ourselves, as did St. Paul.

Devotion to Mary

*I*t is necessary to do three things in honor of Mary:

1. *Know her*, and this means to instruct ourselves
about her virtues, privileges, and greatness;
about the graces she loves to grant;
about her life and her teachings,
and particularly about the events
of her life which better demonstrate to
what heights of grace and merit
our heavenly Mother ascended....

2. *Imitate her*.... Let us look at her and imitate her.

3. *Pray to her*. In all her images Mary is represented as Mother of God,

Refuge of sinners and Dispensatrix of
>   graces,
who obtains light, sanctity, and
merit for us from the Lord.

Love for Mary

*T*oward Mary we must have
an enlightened and limitless
confidence and love;
the most heartfelt,
expansive, and tender devotion;
the most common and constant practices
of the Rosary, the Angelus,
the three Hail Mary's, the chaplet,
> Saturday, etc.*

She must be honored by writing about her,
by preaching about her,
and by giving the example of devotion to her.

---

* This refers to three practices that Alberione encouraged: 1) to pray three Hail Mary's before retiring and upon waking; 2) to pray a chaplet which consists of the prayer "Virgin Mary, Mother of Jesus, make us saints"; and 3) to honor Mary on Saturdays according to the Church's traditional practice.

Mary Reflects Jesus

Mary is a masterpiece of sanctity;
she reflects the virtues of Jesus Christ.
But her sanctity is the simplest,
devoid of those clamorous works
which dazzle and stupefy.
It is a sanctity which can be imitated
in all states of life and in all conditions.

The Queen-Mother

The Queen of the Apostles
is a "Queen-Mother."
Her role as Queen
must not give us the idea only of
a highly exalted creature...no.
On the one hand,
she is Queen so as to be
very rich in grace;
on the other hand,
she is Mother so as to have
a heart full of goodness.

The Greatest Gift

Mary brought the world
the greatest good.
Let us learn from her
how to do good to the world.

The Rosary

Without the Rosary,
he felt incapable
of even making an exhortation.*

---

*Blessed Alberione refers to himself here in the third person in an autobiographical text written at the request of his confreres.

Take Advantage of Mary's Help

To exclude Mary from the apostolate
would be to ignore
one of the most essential parts of
God's redemptive plan.
We would deprive ourselves
of the powerful intercession of Mary.
The apostle, the preacher, the missionary,
the confessor, and the person of action
run a serious risk of building on sand
if their activity does not rest
on an intense devotion to Mary and trust
   in her.

Ask for Mary's Protection

We cannot bring any apostolate to a conclusion
without Mary.
If you want the apostolate to flourish,
place Mary as Queen over it.
Jesus must come, but Mary precedes him—
Mary...became the Mother of Jesus,
whom she then manifested to the world.
Place your apostolate under the
protection of Mary.

Mary and the Family

Mary always comes with both spiritual and maternal blessings. In Zechariah's house she served as the "humble handmaid of the Lord" for three months. And so, for the first time, Jesus reigned in a family with his grace. Later, at the beginning of Jesus' public ministry, Mary entered the newlyweds' house at Cana and obtained the transformation of water into wine. It was there that the first disciples believed in Jesus, who with this miracle had shown himself to be Messiah and God.

A good mother is a great treasure in a family. In a home, Mary acts as the best mother would; in fact, she does more than the best mother could.

Mary brings a human smile and heavenly joy, even where sorrow has entered in.

Mary brings her heavenly light, which peacefully touches persons, even where there is darkness and ignorance.

Mary softens hearts, inclines them toward good, sanctifies traditions, spreads kindness among everyone.

Mary grants understanding and affection between spouses, docility to children, patience and industriousness to everyone.

Through Mary, faith is revived, hope in heaven is strengthened, charity is diffused, and the Christian life is established in a home.

Let us think of Mary's role in the family of Nazareth.

It is therefore to one's greatest advantage to consecrate one's family to the Blessed Virgin, inviting Mary to come and dwell in the home and be a Mother to everyone.

Consecration of the Family to Mary

Come, O Mary,
come and dwell in this home
which we offer and consecrate to you.
You are the welcome one;
we, your children, receive you with joy.
We are unworthy,
but you are so full of goodness
that you willingly make your home
with the poorest of your children.
We welcome you with the same affection
with which St. John brought you into his home
after the death of your Jesus.
Obtain for each one of us the spiritual graces
that we need, just as you brought them
to Zechariah's home.

Obtain for us material graces,
just as you obtained
the transformation of water into wine
for the newlyweds in Cana.
Keep sin far from us, always.
Be for us light, joy, sanctification,
as you were in the family of Nazareth.
Be here for us, Mother, Teacher, and
    Queen.
Increase in us faith, hope, and charity.
Deepen our spirit of prayer.
May Jesus, Way, Truth, and Life, always
    dwell here!
Inspire vocations among our dear ones.
May all the members of this family
be reunited in heaven.

My Soul Magnifies Mary

*M*y soul magnifies Mary,
and my spirit rejoices in my Mother,
Queen, and Teacher.
Because God has regarded
the lowliness of his handmaid:
behold, angels and all people call her
    blessed.
Because he who is mighty
has done great things in her,
and chose her Immaculate, Virgin,
    Mother,
and assumed her into heaven.
The mercy of Mary extends
from one generation to another,
to those who love her and seek her.
The power, the wisdom, and the love of
    Mary

save those who are humble
in the depths of their hearts.
She draws to herself
all those who contemplate her,
those who run
to the perfume of her ointments.
She fills the hungry with good,
to the blind she gives light of heart.
She gave to the world Jesus Master,
who is the blessed fruit of her womb.
And he became the wisdom of God for us,
justice, sanctification, and redemption
throughout the centuries.

The Sixteen Blessings Brought by Mary, Queen of Apostles

1. Mary, Queen of Apostles, will inspire vocations in the families consecrated to her.

2. Mary, Queen of Apostles, will assist the vocations of the parishes and of the dioceses where her image is honored.

3. Mary, Queen of Apostles, will bless the families that give a son or daughter to the Lord.

4. Mary, Queen of Apostles, will smooth the way for those called to the apostolate during the period of their formation.

5. Mary, Queen of Apostles, will form the souls of those called according to the model of Jesus, the first Apostle.

6. Mary, Queen of Apostles, says: I work with everyone who promotes my honor.

7. Mary, Queen of Apostles, blesses everyone

who understands and lives the saying: "Through Mary to Jesus."

8. Mary, Queen of Apostles, protects everyone who works with profound love for Jesus Christ and for the Church.

9. Mary, Queen of Apostles, today offers greater graces to those who work in the more fruitful modern apostolates.

10. Mary, Queen of Apostles, will give to priests who are devoted to her wisdom and efficacy of word.

11. Mary, Queen of Apostles, will sow comfort and joy in the work of the apostolate.

12. Mary, Queen of Apostles, will bless the apostolic work of individuals and of groups.

13. Mary, Queen of Apostles, will sanctify and obtain special blessings for those who make her known and loved.

14. Mary, Queen of Apostles, will assist those

devoted to her throughout their lives and at the hour of their death.

15. Mary, Queen of Apostles, will intercede for them if they are being purified before their entrance into heaven.

16. Mary, Queen of Apostles, will assemble every apostle around her throne of glory in heaven.

Brief Consecration to Mary

I am all yours,
and all that I possess
I offer to you,
my lovable Jesus,
through Mary, your most holy Mother.

Mary Reigns Over Our Hearts

Mary reigns
over our hearts
which she attracts,
molds, and enriches
through the grace of the Holy Spirit.

With Mary

With Mary
everything is easier,
everything is happier,
everything is more fruitful,
everything is holier.
Let us consecrate ourselves to her.

Give Mary Everything

Consecrate to the Queen of Apostles
your mind, your will, your heart,
your fatigue, your work.
Let us consecrate everything to Mary!

Mary Cares for Those Who Stray

Mary does not cease to be our Mother
because we are sinners.
With the Church let us say to her,
"Pray for us sinners."
Let us invoke her,
for she will grant our requests.

No Greater Wealth

We can give no greater wealth
to this poor and proud world
than Jesus Christ.
Mary gave the world grace in Jesus
    Christ;
she goes on offering him down the ages...
she is our Mother.
The world needs Jesus Christ,
Way, Truth, and Life.
[Mary] gives him through apostles
and their apostolates.
She raises them up, instructs them, assists
    them,
and crowns them with good results
and glory in heaven.

Mary and the Apostles

When Jesus returned to heaven,
Mary joined the Apostles in the upper room,
where they waited to receive the Holy Spirit.
She guided the Apostles in prayer and
encouraged them to hope in Jesus' promise
to send his Holy Spirit,
reminding them that it was up to them
to ask Jesus for this gift.
The Bible says that they all
"gathered together in one place"
and that "Mary, the Mother of Jesus, was with them."
She guided the Apostles

not by assuming a role of authority
but through the role of spiritual Mother.
As a result, the Apostles received the
    Holy Spirit
and Mary received this gift
even more abundantly than they did.

Mary, Seat of Wisdom

For how many persons
has Mary been the guiding light!
How many young people
she has helped in their doubts,
and in difficulties with their studies!
Mary is like a serene sky
always lit up by the Divine Sun.
She is always disposed to receive
the splendor of his rays and
transmit the light into the minds of those
who are looking for God and for
    salvation.

A Pact with Mary

A kind of pact must exist
between Mary and us....
It seems to me that this is the most
 fitting:
"Set me as a seal upon your heart,
as a seal upon your arm" (Song 8:6).
It is a seal of love, a strong seal,
because love is strong as death....
To set Mary as a seal upon our heart
means to set devotion to Our Lady
as a seal upon our whole life;
that is, to live in such a way
that she is always before us,
presiding over our studies, our spiritual
 work,
our apostolate: that she be always present
in our entire life.

The Picture of Mary, Queen

The picture of Mary, Queen of Apostles,
precisely represents her in the office,
in the mission, that she had:
to give Jesus to the world.
She is holding Jesus, not tightly to
 herself,
but offering him as light to all who pass
 by.
He carries the scroll of the Gospel,
the Word of life.
With his right hand he is gesturing
with two fingers;
in the first centuries this indicated not so
 much
a blessing as it did the authority of the
 teacher,
who explains wisdom.

And what must you accomplish
in the world by representing Mary,
by imitating Mary? First, interior
 holiness,
and then, giving Jesus to the world....

A Total "Yes"

*M*ary responded
totally to God.
We, too,
must respond
in the same way.

*Prayer for the Ministers of the Word**

O Mary,
you who gave birth
to the Word made flesh,
be present among us:
assist, inspire, and comfort
the ministers of the Word.
O Mary,
you who are Queen of the Apostles,
intervene with your protection
that the light of the Gospel
may reach all peoples.

O Mary,
Mother of Jesus, Way, Truth, and Life,
intercede for us,
so that heaven may be filled
with those who sing the hymn of glory
to the most Holy Trinity.

---

* This is the last Marian prayer that Fr. Alberione wrote at the end of his life when he was almost blind.

Mother of Our Vocation

Mary, the Mother of holy vocations,
is the Mother of your vocation.
She gave the world the greatest Vocation,
the One who was called by the Father
for the sake of all humanity.
In the same way, Mary calls you
and many others
to follow Jesus.

The Picture of the Queen of the Apostles

*I*n the "Hail, Holy Queen,"
the Church describes Mary to us
with very beautiful titles.
The most beautiful, however,
is the one we see portrayed
in the new painting of the
Queen of the Apostles,
in which the Madonna
does not clasp Jesus to her heart,
but holds him out to the Apostles
as her most sweet fruit,
in order that they, in turn, will hold him
    out to humanity.

As Queen, Mary Serves

Mary acted like a servant
in Elizabeth's house.
She put herself at the service of
 Elizabeth,
who, already advanced in age,
was in a delicate condition.
In those circumstances
Mary served her
as a humble handmaid
for three months.

Since 1976, **Marianne Lorraine Trouvé, FSP,** has been a member of the Daughters of St. Paul, an international congregation of women religious dedicated to communicating Christ with the means of communication. She has an M.A. in theology with a concentration in Marian studies from the University of Dayton. She has carried out the Pauline mission through direct apostolic outreach, and since 1994 has served on the editorial staff of Pauline Books & Media. Most recently she has written a pamphlet on the Rosary entitled *Praying the Mysteries of Light*. She also enjoys growing tomatoes in the convent garden.

Pauline
BOOKS & MEDIA

The Daughters of St. Paul operate book and media centers at the following addresses. Visit, call or write the one nearest you today, or find us on the World Wide Web, www.pauline.org

CALIFORNIA
3908 Sepulveda Blvd, Culver City, CA 90230	310-397-8676
5945 Balboa Avenue, San Diego, CA 92111	858-565-9181
46 Geary Street, San Francisco, CA 94108	415-781-5180

FLORIDA
145 S.W. 107th Avenue, Miami, FL 33174	305-559-6715

HAWAII
1143 Bishop Street, Honolulu, HI 96813	808-521-2731
Neighbor Islands call:	866-521-2731

ILLINOIS
172 North Michigan Avenue, Chicago, IL 60601	312-346-4228

LOUISIANA
4403 Veterans Memorial Blvd, Metairie, LA 70006	504-887-7631

MASSACHUSETTS
885 Providence Hwy, Dedham, MA 02026	781-326-5385

MISSOURI
9804 Watson Road, St. Louis, MO 63126	314-965-3512

NEW JERSEY
561 U.S. Route 1, Wick Plaza, Edison, NJ 08817	732-572-1200

NEW YORK
150 East 52nd Street, New York, NY 10022	212-754-1110
78 Fort Place, Staten Island, NY 10301	718-447-5071

PENNSYLVANIA
9171-A Roosevelt Blvd, Philadelphia, PA 19114	215-676-9494

SOUTH CAROLINA
243 King Street, Charleston, SC 29401	843-577-0175

TENNESSEE
4811 Poplar Avenue, Memphis, TN 38117	901-761-2987

TEXAS
114 Main Plaza, San Antonio, TX 78205	210-224-8101

VIRGINIA
1025 King Street, Alexandria, VA 22314	703-549-3806

CANADA
3022 Dufferin Street, Toronto, ON M6B 3T5	416-781-9131
1155 Yonge Street, Toronto, ON M4T 1W2	416-934-3440